B Is for Belonging

Shannon Anderson • illustrated by John Joven

free spirit
PUBLISHING®

Library of Congress Cataloging-in-Publication Data
Names: Anderson, Shannon, 1972- author. | Joven, John, illustrator.
Title: B is for belonging / Shannon Anderson ; illustrated by John Joven.
Description: Minneapolis, MN : Free Spirit Publishing, an imprint of Teacher Created Materials, [2024] | Audience: Ages 4–8.
Identifiers: LCCN 2023053137 (print) | LCCN 2023053138 (ebook) | ISBN 9798885543873 (hardcover) | ISBN 9798885543880 (ebook) |
    ISBN 9798885543897 (epub)
Subjects: LCSH: Belonging (Social psychology) in children—Juvenile literature. | BISAC: JUVENILE NONFICTION / Social Topics / Values & Virtues |
    JUVENILE NONFICTION / Social Topics / Emotions & Feelings
Classification: LCC BF723.B45 A53 2024 (print) | LCC BF723.B45 (ebook) | DDC 302.3085—dc23/eng/20240307
LC record available at https://lccn.loc.gov/2023053137
LC ebook record available at https://lccn.loc.gov/2023053138

Edited by Alison Behnke
Cover and interior design by Courtenay Fletcher
Illustrated by John Joven

Printed by: 70548
Printed in: China
PO#: 11570

Free Spirit Publishing
An imprint of Teacher Created Materials
9850 51st Avenue North, Suite 100
Minneapolis, MN 55442
(612) 338-2068
help4kids@freespirit.com
freespirit.com

FSC
www.fsc.org
MIX
Paper | Supporting
responsible forestry
FSC® C144853

Dedicated to my dear friend Christy Fleming—
an amazing friend, parent, and role model for
compassion and kindness.
—SA

To my amazing friend D!
—JJ

What does it mean to belong? Belonging is about getting to be YOU in a class, a family, a group, and the world. Everyone belongs here!

This is different from fitting in—and it's *way* better. When people try to "fit in," they often think they have to be like someone else to be a part of a group. But you don't have to change yourself to belong or be included.

 **Aa**

When you **accept** other people without judging them or asking them to change, you help them know that they belong.

When you are welcomed and loved exactly as you are, you feel that you belong. **Belonging** feels safe. It helps us be confident and brave.

When you **care** about others, you want them to be happy, loved, and safe. One way to show that you care about someone is to listen to them. We all want to be heard.

You have the power to **decide** how you will treat others. You can choose kind and caring actions.

Having **empathy** means being able to imagine and understand other people's feelings. One way to be empathetic is by asking yourself, "How would I feel if I were in this person's situation?"

All people have **feelings**. It is okay to feel happy, sad, mad, excited, disappointed, and everything in between. Feelings are one way we explore the world and learn from our experiences.

Gg

Each of us has unique **gifts** we can share with the world. Your gifts are not like anyone else's, and that's a good thing. Everyone has something special to give.

You are a **human**—and being human isn't always easy! When you're having a hard day, you can ask for help. And when someone else needs help, you can be there for them. We are all humans, and we can figure out challenges together.

I i

You can **invite** others to spend time with you and to share about their lives, thoughts, feelings, and things they like to do. Learning about others shows that you care about getting to know them.

You can **join** activities with people of all backgrounds and interests. Be part of a club or sport with a group of people you don't know yet. These connections help build strong relationships.

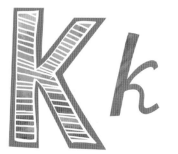

K k

Kindness is a loving way to show you care.
You will never regret being kind.

Even when you don't agree with someone,
you can still show them **love** and respect.

Remembering that we all make **mistakes** helps us forgive ourselves and others. Mistakes help us grow and learn how to make different choices. They actually make us better!

Each of us has different **needs**. Take time to notice the people around you. What do they need? How do they feel? How can you learn from them—and how can they learn from you?

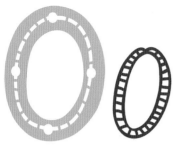

Every day is a new **opportunity** to make friends with people of all ages, genders, abilities, and cultures. You can learn from everyone you meet.

JOIN OUR BIRDWATCHING CLUB

You have the **potential** to do big things.
Potential is your ability to do, make, or be something.
For example, we all have the potential to develop new
friendships, hobbies, and skills.

P p

Qq

You are on a **quest** to learn, grow, and discover more about yourself, other people, and the world. That is what humans do best! This quest is like an adventure for your brain.

We can build strong **relationships** with each other by learning how to talk, listen, and work together. Relationships connect us to others in positive, caring ways.

S s

You can **stand up** for others. If you see someone being treated unkindly or unfairly, you can help them feel safe. This is one of the strongest and bravest ways to show someone that they matter and that you care about their feelings.

When someone is **thoughtful**, they take time to wonder how others think and feel. Part of being thoughtful is thinking about others' needs and trying to respect those needs.

U u

Knowing that other people **understand** you helps you feel like you belong. And when you try to understand other people's experiences, it helps you be a better friend. Being understood and heard helps you feel accepted for who you are.

TALES FROM SPACE!

You have a unique and powerful **voice**.
You can use your voice to lift up others, to
encourage yourself, and to do big things!

Every person is **worthy** of love and compassion. You don't have to do anything but be you in order to be loved. Your worth is not tied to what you look like or how others see you.

We each have one e**X**traordinary life.
We can make a difference in this world by helping
others feel that they matter—because they do!

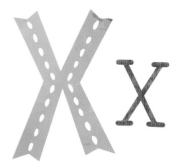

Yy

You are the best YOU, and a precious human.
Be loving to yourself and accepting of yourself.

There are a **zillion** ways to be you, and a zillion ways to belong. Everyone is unique—and that is part of what makes our world so interesting!

What will you do today to show acceptance for others and yourself?
Who can you try to include?
What about yourself are you most proud of?

We all feel amazing, important, and included when others accept us, love us, and welcome us. And each of us can spread this feeling by helping others know they belong too. We all belong!

Activities to Build Empathy and Belonging

You can use the activities in this section to foster and strengthen a sense of belonging among the children you spend time with—whether you're a teacher, counselor, family member, or other caring adult. Feel free to adapt these in ways that work best for your group. (Most of these activities also work well if you're reading the book one-on-one!) Building empathy and belonging leads to greater levels of self-esteem, a stronger sense of self-identity, and better peer relationships. Helping all kids feel that they are valued, seen, heard, and safe improves their academic, social, and emotional outcomes. What could be better than that?

Share and Care

When we share items we care about, it opens up conversation and allows us to get to know each other better. We can appreciate everyone for their interests and passions.

Invite children to share an item that means a lot to them. Give each child the opportunity to show their item and tell why it is special. Perhaps it has significance in their family or culture or it belongs to a collection they treasure. It could be that it was given to them by a special person in their life, or maybe they created the item themselves. Invite respectful questions and conversation from the group.

Reaching by Teaching

When children teach each other, they get to share their unique talents. In turn, kids develop mutual appreciation for their peers and their various abilities. You can have pairs teach each other one-on-one or allow children to take turns teaching the entire group.

Have children choose something they could teach to others. This could be making an origami frog, doing a card trick, using a particular app, showing how to draw something, or just about anything else that can be taught in 10 to 15 minutes! Be sure to give children time to prepare and gather items they may need. In the case of demonstrations that involve pets, cooking, or specialized equipment, you may want to give them the option to film themselves at home and share the video.

The "You're Special!" Project

It feels good to know that others appreciate us—and it also feels good to show our appreciation for others. By giving children the chance to offer and receive compliments and affirmation, this activity serves as a powerful morale-booster and showcases how all of us are special and wonderful in our own unique ways.

This project is best begun after your group has already had some time to get to know each other. Explain that the "You're Special!" project is a way for them to share kind words and authentic compliments, creating an environment where everyone feels welcomed and accepted exactly as they are. Be sure to take time to explain what it means to give thoughtful, sincere affirmations. They should be as specific and personalized as possible. Also encourage children to focus on admirable talents, skills, attitudes, and personality traits rather than appearance or other more superficial qualities. For example, children might say why they are thankful to have someone else in the group, share a memory of a positive interaction with them, or describe ways they help others. You can brainstorm some ideas as a group (perhaps about someone who is in the community but not part of your group) and then work to make the compliments stronger so children understand how to craft authentic and meaningful compliments.

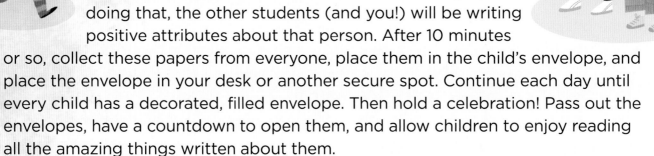

Once children understand the concept, spend a few minutes every day on the "You're Special!" project until you have written compliments and affirmations for everyone in your group. Each day, randomly choose one child to decorate an envelope for themselves using crayons, markers, stickers, and so on. While they are doing that, the other students (and you!) will be writing positive attributes about that person. After 10 minutes or so, collect these papers from everyone, place them in the child's envelope, and place the envelope in your desk or another secure spot. Continue each day until every child has a decorated, filled envelope. Then hold a celebration! Pass out the envelopes, have a countdown to open them, and allow children to enjoy reading all the amazing things written about them.

Belonging Versus Fitting In

Belonging and fitting in can seem alike, but belonging is **so** much better. This activity helps kids to understand that idea by considering example scenarios. It also enables children to more easily recognize when someone is trying to pressure them to change in order to fit in. And that understanding, in turn, helps build self-acceptance, self-confidence, and resistance to peer pressure.

Begin by having a discussion about what children think the differences are between belonging and fitting in. Invite them to share experiences with and examples of each. You can ask some questions to get this going, such as:

- What does belonging mean to you?
- How is "fitting in" different than belonging?
- Where is a place you know you belong?
- What is a time when you've felt you had to change for others to like you?
- How can you tell if someone is excluding you?

Take notes during this discussion. Based on your group's ideas, needs, and questions, create a deck of cards, with each card displaying a short sentence that describes either belonging or fitting in. Make sure there is an equal number of cards in each category, and create at least one card per child. However, don't label cards with their category. Instead, children will discuss and decide what the cards describe. Here are some examples of what cards might say:

Belonging Cards

- I feel confident sharing my ideas.
- My friends say nice things to me.
- I feel safe.
- I can wear what I like.
- People respect my opinions.
- I feel comfortable.
- I can try new things.
- I know my friends care about me.
- I can be honest about my feelings.
- I can be myself.

Fitting In Cards

- I feel like people ignore me.
- I worry about being made fun of.
- I don't feel confident sharing my ideas.
- People in my group put me down.
- I don't feel comfortable being myself.
- Sometimes my friends laugh at me.
- I don't always feel safe in my group.
- People get mad if I don't agree with them.
- I feel pressured to act or dress a certain way.
- I don't feel like my opinion matters.

Next, mix up the cards and pass them out. When everyone has a card, have children move around the room and compare their cards. If they think their card describes belonging, ask them to look for someone whose card describes fitting in. Then invite each pair to talk about the ideas on their cards. They could discuss how the ideas are different, share a time when they had the experience being described, or brainstorm ways to respond to being pressured to fit in. As needed, rotate through the space to guide children toward productive and respectful conversation.

To extend this activity further, children could role-play scenarios based on the cards' prompts.

Handprint Poem

This creative activity produces artwork showing how each of us is unique, from our handprints to our feelings.

First, using nontoxic, washable paints, have each child make a colorful handprint on a piece of cardstock or art paper.

Next, as the paint dries, have children create affirming poems about themselves by prompting them with sentence starters like the following:

- I love . . .
- I'm excited about . . .
- I'm proud of . . .
- I worry about . . .
- Someday, I hope to . . .
- I wonder about . . .
- I'm good at . . .

Finally, when the painted handprint pages are dry, have children write their sentences in the space around their handprints (with your help if necessary). If children also want to decorate their handprint poems with drawings, stickers, or other elements, they may.

Last but not least, display the artwork as a reminder that each of us is special, and all of us belong.

For more activity ideas, download a Leader's Guide at go.freespirit.com/leader.

About the Author and Illustrator

Shannon Anderson is an award-winning children's book author, TEDx speaker, and national presenter. She loves to do author visits in classrooms to teach the power of reading, writing, and learning with a growth mindset. Shannon taught for 25 years from first grade through college level, where she wore the hats of literacy coach, gifted coordinator, and adjunct professor. She lives in Indiana. You can learn more about Shannon and her books at shannonisteaching.com.

John Joven is an illustrator and a painter from Colombia. He lives there with his wife, Ana, and two children, Avril and Ian. He is fortunate enough to work in his home studio, where he can share his passion for drawing and painting with his children while working on projects. He started drawing at an early age, and when he was six years old his parents enrolled him in his first painting, sculpture, and character design class. When not illustrating, he enjoys spending time with his family, playing soccer with friends, watching movies, reading, writing, and traveling. He has had the opportunity to bring to life characters, scenes, and diverse worlds in magazines and newspapers; funny ideas in children's books; and animation projects around the globe.

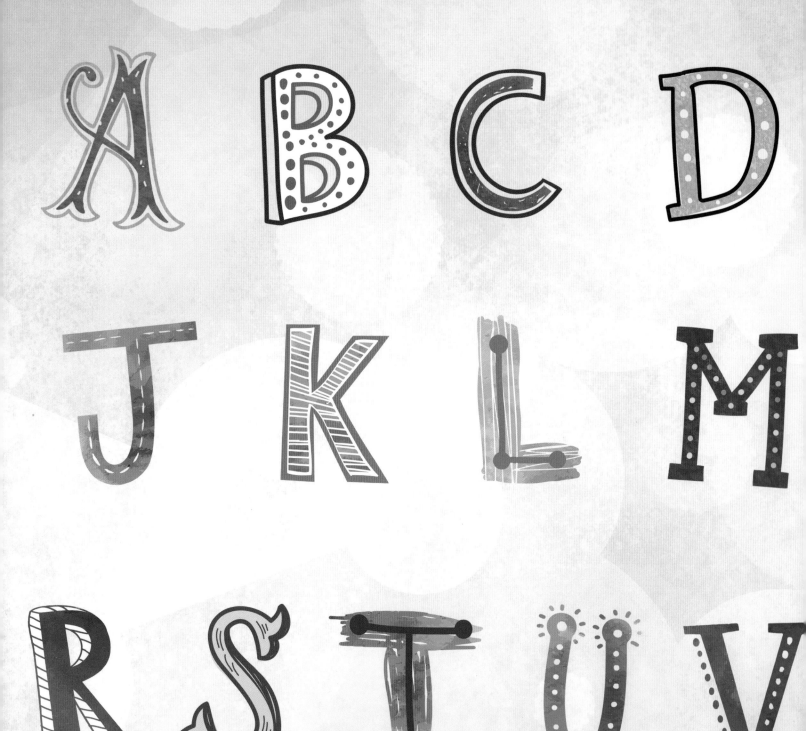